Beyoncé

by Z.B. Hill

Superstars of Hip-Hop

Alicia Keys

Beyoncé

Black Eyed Peas

Ciara

Dr. Dre

Drake

Eminem

50 Cent

Flo Rida

Hip Hop:
A Short History

Jay-Z

Kanye West

Lil Wayne

LL Cool J

Ludacris

Mary J. Blige

Notorious B.I.G.

Rihanna

Sean "Diddy" Combs

Snoop Dogg

T.I.

T-Pain

Timbaland

Tupac

Usher

Beyoncé

by Z.B. Hill

Mason Crest

Beyoncé

Mason Crest
370 Reed Road
Broomall, Pennsylvania 19008
www.masoncrest.com

Printed and bound in the United States of America.

First printing
9 8 7 6 5 4 3 2 1

Library of Congress Cataloging-in-Publication Data

Hill, Z. B.
 Beyoncé / by Z. B. Hill.
    p. cm. – (Superstars of hip hop)
  ISBN 978-1-4222-2510-3 (hardcover) – ISBN 978-1-4222-2508-0 (series hardcover) – ISBN 978-1-4222-9212-9 (ebook)
 1. Beyoncé, 1981–-Juvenile literature. 2. Singers–United States–Biography–Juvenile literature. I. Title.
 ML3930.K66H55 2012
 782.42164092–dc22
 [B]
                                    2011005425

Produced by Harding House Publishing Services, Inc.
www.hardinghousepages.com
Interior Design by MK Bassett-Harvey.
Cover design by Torque Advertising & Design.

Publisher's notes:
• All quotations in this book come from original sources and contain the spelling and grammatical inconsistencies of the original text.
• The Web sites mentioned in this book were active at the time of publication. The publisher is not responsible for Web sites that have changed their addresses or discontinued operation since the date of publication. The publisher will review and update the Web site addresses each time the book is reprinted.

DISCLAIMER: The following story has been thoroughly researched, and to the best of our knowledge, represents a true story. While every possible effort has been made to ensure accuracy, the publisher will not assume liability for damages caused by inaccuracies in the data, and makes no warranty on the accuracy of the information contained herein. This story has not been authorized nor endorsed by Beyoncé.

Contents

Hip-Hop lingo

The **Grammy Awards** (short for Gramophone Awards)—or Grammys—are given out each year by the National Academy of Recording Arts and Sciences to people who have done something really big in the music industry.

Talent shows are contests where people compete to show how good they are at something.

A **professional** is someone who gets paid money to do something she's good at.

A **manager** is someone who helps and guides a musician.

Chapter 1

The Beginning

Big Night

January 31, 2010 was a big night for Beyoncé, one of the biggest nights of her life. It was the night of the 2010 **Grammy Awards**. She performed for a room packed full of famous people. She danced, sang, and won six Grammys. Try to picture her—smiling out at a cheering audience, breathing hard as she tries to catch her breath. Watching Beyoncé that night, it's hard to imagine that she was once a shy little girl. But believe it or not, she was.

The Beginning

Beyoncé was born on September 4, 1981, in Houston, Texas. Her proud parents were Tina and Mathew Knowles. Her mom chose her first name, Beyoncé, and her dad chose her middle name, Giselle. She was Beyoncé Giselle Knowles—a beautiful name for a beautiful daughter.

Not long after Beyoncé was born, her parents had another baby girl. They named her Solange. Beyoncé now had a sister, and their family was complete.

Tina Knowles owned a hair salon when Beyoncé was a child. Beyoncé worked in her mom's salon, even singing to the customers. Here Beyoncé and her mother share their love of fashion, attending the CFDA Fashion Awards in 2004.

The Beginning

Beyoncé's parents worked hard to give their daughters the best. Beyoncé's mom, Tina, owned a hair salon. Her dad, Mathew, sold medical supplies. But that wasn't always his job. In the 1960s and '70s, Mathew had fought hard for African American rights. Now, in the '80s, he was ready to fight for his family instead. Mathew and Tina made sure their two daughters had everything they needed. Both girls went to private school, and they lived in a nice home.

When Beyoncé's parents were kids, they loved to sing. Mathew and Tina sang in their school chorus and did **talent shows**, too. They never got paid money to sing, but they loved it anyway. They wanted to pass that love on to their daughters. A favorite family activity was to gather around the piano. Mathew played, and Tina and the two girls sang along.

Beyoncé loved to sing. She was good at it, too. By the time she was in first grade, she had made up her mind. She wanted to be a singer when she grew up. Her parents were excited about their daughter's talent. They did everything they could to help her.

The song she sang at her first talent show was John Lennon's "Imagine." When Beyoncé's parents heard her sing, they were amazed. They knew their daughter had a beautiful voice. Her dad decided to help her become a **professional** singer. He started a singing group for her with five other girls. They called it Girls Tyme.

The six little girls practiced their singing all the time. They signed up for talent shows all over the state of Texas. Each time they sang and got awards, Beyoncé got a little closer to her dream of becoming a professional singer.

Hard Times

By the time Beyoncé was eleven years old, she and her father both felt she was ready for fame. They were excited when they found out about a TV show called *Star Search. Star Search* invited young

9

people to show off their talent and get prizes. Christina Aguilera and Britney Spears got famous on *Star Search*. Beyoncé hoped she would too.

Then great news came. *Star Search* invited Girls Tyme to be on the show. Beyoncé, her dad, and the other girls in Girls Tyme were very excited. They were nervous too. They didn't want to mess it up!

When the big day came, the six girls went to the TV studio. They stood in the dark room next to the stage. They waited for their turn to go on. Finally, someone called their name—"Girls Tyme!" The six girls walked out with smiles on their faces and their hearts beating fast. They sang the best they could.

But the judges had bad news for them. Beyoncé forced herself to smile as she listened. The judges gave them only three out of five stars. The girls sang well, but the song they chose wasn't very good. They had sung their best, but their best wasn't good enough. Beyoncé cried as she walked backstage.

The blow was too much for some of the girls. A few quit the group and gave up. But Mathew Knowles didn't give up. He helped Beyoncé form a new group of four girls. He stood beside his daughter all the way.

Parents to the Rescue

Mathew Knowles saw that his daughter needed more help. He quit his job and became a full-time **manager** for Beyoncé. She told *Ebony* magazine: "My father . . . would always book shows for us. We would try to perform once a week, and in the summer, twice a week. I'm very lucky. Both my parents support me and my career."

Both her parents gave up a lot of time and energy for Beyoncé. When Mathew quit his job, the family had less money. Beyoncé's parents sold their home and their cars. They moved into a smaller apartment. Mathew managed the group, and Tina made their costumes and styled their hair.

They still had a long way to go. Over the next few years, the girls gave their group a bunch of different names. They tried Something Fresh, Cliché, The Dolls, and Destiny. Finally they chose Destiny's Child. The name felt right, so they kept it.

Mathew Knowles has been a driving force in Beyoncé's career. The salesman quit his job to manage his daughter's and Destiny's Child's careers. In 2004, he and Beyonce attended the 46th Annual Grammy Awards, where his dedication was rewarded with Beyoncé's five awards.

Those were important years for the group. While the girls practiced, Tina Knowles tried her best to make her business better. The hair salon became another way for the girls to practice their skills. They performed for Tina's customers, singing songs while ladies had their hair styled.

Beyoncé's adolescence was filled with many of the same insecurities felt by most teens. She was very shy, she wore braces and glasses, she was chubby. But Beyoncé worked through those growing pains to become a successful and happy singer, actress, and person.

Growing Pains

Meanwhile, Beyoncé was growing up. It wasn't easy. The Beyoncé we see on TV seems so confident and outgoing. But when she was a kid, she was very quiet and shy. She was a normal girl with normal worries. School was hard for her. She wore braces and glasses. She was a little chubby, and she was afraid to speak out loud in her classes. Beyoncé was very different then from the woman we see on stage today!

But Beyoncé had a secret. Whenever she felt scared to go on stage, or to sing in front of a group, she pretended to be someone else. She pretended to be a girl named Sasha. Sasha was never afraid. Beyoncé might be shy, but Sasha was loud and proud.

Beyoncé lived two lives. In one, she was a quiet girl who didn't talk a lot. In the other, she was a talented singer. She had good reasons for not telling people she could sing. Kids at school thought she was stuck-up because she didn't talk a lot. Beyoncé didn't want to make things worse by telling them about her talent.

Life at home was a different story. She practiced for hours every night. Some nights, she spent as many as eight hours working on her songs. She dreamed of becoming a famous singer.

And she was not going to stop until the dream came true.

Hip-Hop lingo

A **record** is a group of songs played on a plastic disc by a phonograph. Today CDs have replaced records.

The **opening act** is a musical group that goes on stage before another musical group.

To **tour** means to travel around and play music for people at concerts.

An **album** has a bunch of songs made to go together.

A **single** is a really popular song from an album that's released first by itself.

Number-one hits are songs that are so popular that they become the most-listened-to songs in the country.

A **lawsuit** is when someone accuses someone else of something and brings them to court.

Billboard is a magazine that keeps track of which songs are most popular.

Chapter 2

Destiny's Child
Is Born

Destiny Child Gets Started

Everything seemed to happen at once for Destiny's Child. Their hard work began to pay off. They finally had a group name that everyone loved. They were singing better than ever. They were ready for the next step.

In 1997, they took that step. Destiny's Child signed a **record** deal with Columbia Records. A record deal means a company will pay for a music group to make songs. If the songs become popular and sell a lot, the group gets some of the money, while the music company gets the rest.

Right away, Destiny's Child made some great songs. Everyone knew there was something special about this group. They made a song called "Killing Time" for the movie *Men in Black.* People loved it. Christina Aguilera, who was really famous, asked them to be her **opening act**. They went on **tour** with her. People across the country got to hear Destiny's Child's music.

The girls moved to Los Angeles and made their first **album**, called *Destiny's Child*. Beyoncé was closer than ever to making her dream come true. Destiny's Child worked hard to make the best album they could. In 1998, the group released their first **single** from the album, called "No, No, No." It was a hit. People loved it!

Beyoncé will never forget the first time she heard one of her songs on the radio. She was on her way to pick up her sister from school. Then she heard the song on the car speakers. She was so excited that she got out and ran around the car screaming "Aaaahhh!" When her sister heard the song, she started screaming too. Beyoncé was on her way to becoming famous. And she was just sixteen years old!

Not All Fun and Games

Those early days were amazing. Every week, Destiny's Child sold more copies of their album. Every week, Beyoncé got closer to her dream. But she had to make a lot of tough choices. Other girls her age had nothing to worry about besides dates and grades. Not Beyoncé. She didn't have time for boys or school. Instead of going to class every day, she had a tutor. A tutor is someone who meets with a student one-on-one. Beyoncé said having a tutor was "very serious and boring."

Sometimes she just wanted to have fun like other kids. She wanted to be a cheerleader, or go to sports games. But she gave up all that stuff to follow her dream.

Writing Songs

Beyoncé turned eighteen in 1999, the same year her group's second album came out. It was called *The Writing's on the Wall*. It was even better than the first. It had two **number-one hits**. One of the hit songs, "Say My Name," won two Grammy Awards.

Beyoncé wasn't just a singer. She was a writer, too. She wrote many of Destiny's Child's songs. She expressed her feelings. She wrote about the pressures of being famous. She felt like people expected her to have a perfect body. So she wrote a song called "Bootylicious." It was a song about loving your body, no matter what size it is.

Michelle Williams and Farrah Franklin replaced LaTavia Roberson and LeToya Luckett when they left Destiny's Child in 2000. After Farrah left, the group became a trio, which they have remained. In this photo (left to right), the final trio of Beyoncé, Michelle, and Kelly are shown recording a track.

Beyoncé found she had a gift. Her songs made people feel better. When she sang, people listened.

Things were going so well. But then everything came to a stop.

The Lawsuit

In 2000, LaTavia and LeToya, two of the members of Destiny's Child, quit the group. Beyoncé was very upset. Then things got worse. The two girls filed a **lawsuit** against Beyoncé's dad, Mathew. They said Mathew treated them unfairly. They said he made Beyoncé more important than Destiny's Child.

In 2001, Destiny's Child's album *Survivor* hit the charts in the number-one spot, and sold more than nine million copies worldwide! The group won two Grammys and many other awards. Beyoncé became the first African American woman to win Songwriter of the Year from ASCAP.

This really hurt Beyoncé. Destiny's Child was like a family for her. Watching the two girls walk away felt like watching her family split up. For a month, she barely left her room. She felt like she used to feel in school—all alone.

But her dad was there to help. Mathew hired two new singers. Their names were Michelle Williams and Farrah Franklin. The new girls started practicing right away. They filmed a music video. They performed at concerts. They did everything that the old girls did. But it was too much work for one of them. After a few months, Farrah quit the group. She was just a teenage girl, and she was tired.

Destiny's Child made a new plan. They decided not to replace Farrah. They became a group of three girls instead of four. Beyoncé was sad again, but she pushed ahead. She went back to work and stayed positive. She was not going to let anything stop her now.

Survivor

Beyoncé had come a long way. She had survived a lot of hard times. So she decided to call her third album *Survivor*. She wrote most of the songs on the album. It was very personal for her. She was telling her story to the world.

The results were amazing. Survivor was number one on the **Billboard** list. It went on to sell more than nine million copies around the world. The album's success proved Beyoncé's talent as a songwriter. She was as creative as she was talented!

That same year Beyoncé received an award all her own. It was the "Songwriter of the Year" award. She was the first African American woman to ever win it.

Things were going great for Destiny's Child. But the girls decided to take a break. They wanted to have their own careers. The next few years would be some of the most exciting in Beyoncé's life.

Hip-Hop lingo

Solo means by yourself. A solo artist sings by herself instead of with a group.

A **star** is a famous person, like an actor or singer, who lots of people know about and like.

A **charity** is a group that gives time, money, or other things to help make people's lives better.

Diabetes is a disease that makes it hard for a person's body to handle sugar.

Chapter 3

Going Solo

The success of Destiny's Child opened up new doors for Beyoncé. She was on the covers of magazines. She was on television almost every day. People wanted to pay her thousands of dollars just to wear their clothes or drink their soda. It was a whole new chapter in Beyoncé's story. Suddenly anything was possible.

New Experiences

So Beyoncé decided she wanted to try acting in movies. She got a part in a movie called *Austin Powers in Goldmember*. Her character's name was Foxxy Cleopatra. Foxxy helped Austin Powers save the world from Dr. Evil.

Beyoncé was very nervous about being an actor. But she did her best anyway. She told someone at BeatBoxBetty.com, "I didn't think what would happen if it went bad. I just did it and tried to do the best I could. I tried to learn. I felt like it was a new chapter of my life, a new way to grow. . . ."

Another Lawsuit

Once again LaTavia and LeToya filed a lawsuit against Beyoncé. They said that Beyoncé wrote mean things about them in the song "Survivor."

Beyoncé was upset. But this time she didn't try to hide it. She let them know how she felt, and then she moved on. She had worked too hard to give up now. After her work for *Goldmember* was done, she returned to singing.

Beyoncé has experienced incredible success and rave reviews as a solo performer. She has performed in front of enthusiastic audiences, like this one in New York City in 2003, and won many awards for her individual efforts.

A lot of people didn't think Beyoncé could make it **solo**. They thought she would fail without Destiny's Child. But they were wrong.

Singing Without Destiny's Child

Beyoncé has one of the best voices in hip-hop. But not everyone knew that in 2003, before her first solo album came out. The more Beyoncé sang alone, though, the more people realized her talent. Her voice is a lot like an opera singer's voice. One magazine put her at number seven for the best "Pop Vocals" of all time.

First Solo Album

Beyoncé's first solo album was called *Dangerously in Love*. The day it came out in 2003 was one of the biggest days of her life. The album had a song on it called "Crazy in Love" with a guest rap from Jay-Z on it. The song stayed for ten weeks at number one. It became one of the summer's biggest hits.

Everyone talked about the album that summer. It sold more than two million copies by the end of the year. People listened to it all over the world. It became number one in England and Canada too.

Beyoncé's first album proved her talent as a solo singer. It won lots of awards and gave Beyoncé more confidence. She decided to do another movie. This time she acted in *The Fighting Temptations*. She also made a song with Missy Elliott for the movie. One magazine said she was one of the best singers of 2003.

Beyoncé was famous. She was on the covers of magazines. She was an actor in three movies. She was no longer just a singer. She was a **star**!

"Crazy in Love" was a huge hit in the summer of 2003. The song also brought Beyoncé a new love, rap legend Jay-Z, who guest rapped on the track. In this photo from 2003, she and Jay-Z are seen performing at the Z-100 Jingle Ball.

Living the Dream

Beyoncé's life was busier than ever. In 2004, she went on tour with Alicia Keys and Missy Elliott.

Life didn't slow down when the tour ended. Everyone wanted some of Beyoncé's time. It was just part of being a star. She did lots of TV shows. She received lots of awards. Suddenly the little girl from Houston was a powerful woman.

In September of 2004, another dream came true. Beyoncé and her mom started a clothing line together. The two women named it after Beyoncé's grandmother, Agnes Deréon. When she was alive, Agnes made clothes for a living. Beyoncé and her mom wanted to carry on Agnes's love of clothes. The clothing line they started became very popular.

Reaching Out to Others

Beyoncé used her fame to help others. She gave some songs to the Texas Music Project CD. The project gave money to music programs in Texas schools. The schools needed the money badly. Beyoncé was happy to help. Music had been a huge part of her childhood, and now, it was the purpose of her whole life. She wanted to give that gift to other kids.

Beyoncé found time to do another **charity** event. This time it was a concert to help kids with **diabetes**. Lots of singers and musicians showed up to support it.

Around the World with Destiny's Child

Beyoncé was not about to slow down. In 2005, she rejoined her friends in Destiny's Child. It was time to tour the world. The group went to Europe, Asia, and back to the United States.

Then they did it again! This time they called their tour "The Destiny Fulfilled . . . and Lovin' It." Everything about the tour was bigger and better. Beyoncé's mom designed the costumes. The stage lights were beautiful. It was Destiny's Child's best tour yet!

The group finished the year with lots of awards. It was a great year for Destiny's Child. They were in Wal-Mart's Christmas ads. The toy company Mattel even made Destiny's Child Barbie dolls!

Beyoncé was a success worldwide. in this 2003 photo, she shows off MTV Europe music awards for Best Song and Best R&B Song. Beyoncé had a phenomenal 2003 and was looking forward to reuniting with Destiny's Child in 2004.

Friends and Family

Beyoncé found the strength she needed. When she didn't find it in herself, she found it in other people. She had pushed herself as hard as she could since she was a little girl. She made it through bad times and good times because of her family and friends. They kept her going strong.

She couldn't do it alone. Lots of people say mean things to you when you're famous. You need friends and family to support you. She told someone at Handbag.com, "I have people who love me . . . whether I sell another record or not."

At the end of the day, Beyoncé knew who loved her. She kept those people close. Two of her cousins traveled with her on tour. Her entire family visits her when she goes far away. Best of all, Beyoncé still had two good friends from Destiny's Child.

Hip-Hop lingo

An **artist** is someone who creates something. Some artists use their voices to make music.

Genres are different types of something, like different types of music.

An **octave** is a group of eight musical notes from low to high. Most people can sing two octaves with their voice.

Lyrics are the words in a song.

Pop is short for "popular." Pop music is usually light and happy, with a good beat.

A **producer** is the person in charge of putting together songs. A producer makes the big decisions about the music.

Beats are the basic rhythms or pulse of a piece of music.

Melodies are the tunes of pieces of music. They are made by arranging musical notes in a pattern.

A **studio** is the place where music gets recorded and made into CDs.

A person who is in the **spotlight** has a lot of public attention on her.

Chapter 4

Beyoncé the Artist

No one knows exactly how to describe Beyoncé's music. She changes her style all the time. Sometimes she sings hip-hop. Other times she sings **genres** like funk or soul. She changes her music to keep things interesting.

Her Voice

Beyoncé's voice helps her succeed in many genres. Many people admire her voice. They say she has a three-and-a-half-**octave** voice. That's amazing for a singer. She can make her voice sound angry, sad, or happy. She can whisper or roar. People connect to the emotions they hear in her voice. Her voice is what allows her to tell stories. It's also a big part of why people love her songs.

Beyoncé's Lyrics

People also love Beyoncé's **lyrics**. Her songs tell how she really feels. Many of the songs she writes are about her own life. Beyoncé had the same boyfriend from the age of twelve to nineteen. He hurt her when he broke up with her. Beyoncé uses her lyrics to talk about personal things like that.

Many **pop** singers let other people write their music and lyrics. But not Beyoncé. She's written music and lyrics for almost every album she's made. People do help her sometimes, but she never sits back and does nothing. She wants her music to be very personal.

Being personal is part of her success. Her lyrics tell the story of a real woman's life. Many of her first songs are about being strong. They're about overcoming hard times. Beyoncé wrote them when Destiny's Child almost broke up for good. She wrote them after her boyfriend broke up with her.

Over time, she has gained a lot of confidence. She became famous. She worked hard to keep her career going and not change into a different person. She married Jay-Z. All these changes led to new emotions. New emotions led to new lyrics.

Beyoncé went through a lot. That helped her reach out and touch people's lives. People connected with these real emotions.

Making Music

Beyoncé is both a **producer** and a songwriter. As a producer, she has a lot of control over her music. She chooses which songs to sing. She decides how she wants them to sound. She picks musicians and **artists** she wants to work with.

Beyoncé does not make **beats** for her songs. She lets other people do that. But she does do other important songwriting work. She usually comes up with **melodies** and ideas on her own. She brings those melodies into the **studio**. Then other songwriters and musicians help her complete the song. They play music for her and try to decide what fits the song.

Beyoncé's Image

When you're a pop star, your image is important. Image is much more than just how you dress or look. Image is how people think

Giving back is important to Beyoncé, and she participates in many charity events. Here she is shown performing in 2004 at the 16th Carousel of Hope Ball, a fund-raising event for the Barbara Davis Center for Childhood Diabetes.

about you. A good or bad image might mean the difference between a career or no career.

Beyoncé has made a very good image for herself. She has very few enemies, which helps a lot. Not many people hate Beyoncé. She's done her best to be kind and not say mean things about anyone. People respect that.

Beyoncé's been in the **spotlight** for over ten years. Being famous is nothing new to her. She's had a long time to learn how to behave in public. She never loses her temper with reporters. She doesn't abuse drugs or alcohol. People respect her for her self-control and good attitude. This makes for a great image.

Live Concerts

A live concert is a show done in person. Beyoncé's live show is one of the best. She has done many tours for her many albums. She's done live shows with Destiny's Child, and she's done them for her solo career. People say she has more energy than almost any other pop singer. Energy is important when you're putting on live shows. Having energy means Beyoncé moves around a lot on stage. She is excited to be there, so the crowd gets excited too.

In 2006, Beyoncé created an all-girl band called Suga Mama. She hired them to come on tour with her and play their instruments for the crowd.

Beyoncé's shows are like magic. She uses smoke and glitter and fire. She wants to give the crowd the time of their lives. There are beautiful costumes and flashing lights. Listening to Beyoncé live is a lot different than listening to her CDs. It's much more of a rush!

Beyoncé and Sasha

Beyoncé still saw herself as two people. When she was little, it was Beyoncé and Sasha. One was shy and the other was confident. As an adult, Beyoncé had a stage-self and a "real-life" self.

For a long time, Beyoncé kept Sasha a secret. She became Sasha only on stage. Sasha had a last name, too—Fierce. She needed Sasha Fierce to do things that she couldn't do. Sometimes, Beyoncé was too scared to sing. Sometimes she didn't want to dance in front of a crowd. But Sasha was always ready.

Beyoncé wanted to take her career to the next level. She wanted to do great live shows. She wanted people to enjoy her concerts. So she used Sasha to bring out a "fierce" side of herself. For Beyoncé, being "fierce" meant a lot of things. "Fierce" is taking action to get what you want. "Fierce" is not being scared. Sasha was "fierce" when Beyoncé was not.

A lot of people didn't understand this. Beyoncé looked different on stage. She wore less clothes and lots of makeup. Some people thought this was who she really was. But Beyoncé knew who she was.

Beyoncé told people not to judge her based on what they saw on stage. She wanted people to see the real her. She didn't want to be misunderstood.

Then Beyoncé released her album *I Am . . . Sasha Fierce*. This was a big move. She finally told the world about her two sides. Beyoncé told someone at *Allure* magazine that she was done being Sasha. She "killed" Sasha when she became Sasha once and for all.

Instead of switching between two people, she became one. She told *Allure*: "I don't need Sasha Fierce anymore. I've grown and now I'm able to merge the two."

Hip-Hop lingo

A **starring role** is one of the most important parts in the movie or television show.

Chapter 5

Getting Personal

Beyoncé's personal life is as busy as her music career. Relationships are very important to Beyoncé. She tries to reach out and touch the lives of others. In 2003, love reached out and touched her when she met Jay-Z. Some people say that Jay-Z is the best rapper alive. For Beyoncé, he's simply the love of her life.

They met for the first time in the fall of 2002. Beyoncé sang on Jay-Z's song "03 Bonnie and Clyde." A few months later, they started dating. Beyoncé had found someone like herself in Jay-Z, whose real name is Sean Carter. When they met, Sean was in charge of a record company. He had made lots of albums, just like Beyoncé.

After dating a while, they got married in 2008. Only nobody knew about it. Strange as it sounds, there were no pictures of their wedding. They kept it a secret. Being famous makes it hard to have privacy, but Beyoncé doesn't like to show her private life to the whole world.

Beyoncé and Jay-Z are almost never seen together. They stay away from cameras. But Beyoncé did thank her husband at the 2010 Grammys, when she got the award for Best Female Vocal Performance. She said, "I'd love to thank my family for all of their support. Including my husband. I love you."

This surprised a lot of people. Beyoncé rarely talks about her husband, Jay-Z. She must have been really happy!

Good News

Beyoncé got a lot of good news in 2011. In June, she released her fourth album, *4*. The album was a huge hit. In its first week, the album reached number one of the Billboard album charts. Fans bought 310,000 copies of *4* in that week alone!

But that wasn't the only good news Beyonce got in 2011. She and husband Jay-Z also found out they were going to have a baby! In January, 2012, Beyonce gave birth to daughter Blue Ivy Carter in New York City. She and Jay-Z couldn't have been happier.

Just a few days later, Jay released a song called "Glory." In the song, he raps about how happy he is to be a father. At the end of "Glory," Jay recorded Blue Ivy crying. He told fans that it was the beginning of her music career. When "Glory" became a hit on the Billboard charts, Blue Ivy Carter became the youngest person ever on the charts!

Beyoncé and Love

Beyoncé says that she is a private person. She doesn't want her love life all over the news. She told Handbag.com, "I'll tell my friends, I just don't feel comfortable telling the whole world."

Love is important to Beyoncé, but it's not everything. She doesn't want to be known only by her connection to a man. She wants to have her own identity.

She also thinks that falling in love takes courage. She told Ya-hoo! Music how she feels about falling in love: "It's letting go and giving your heart to someone else. . . . I know for me, who always tries to be so tough, that's the dangerous thing. That's the hard thing. But it's part of growing up."

Friendships

Beyoncé stayed close to her friends in Destiny's Child. In 2004, the girls got back together to make their album *Destiny Fulfilled*. Then they went on tour in 2005. But this was their last trip around the world.

Even when they took time off from performing together, the members of Destiny's Child stayed close. Their relationship goes much deeper than the group. In 2004, the group reunited for *Destiny Fulfilled*. Here Kelly, Beyoncé, and Michelle reunited shown at the 2005 Fashion Rocks event.

In 2005, Destiny's Child told everyone they were breaking up. They made it clear that they would stay friends, though. A magazine asked Beyoncé if Destiny's Child would ever get back together. She said, "Who knows what will happen in three, five, or ten years? The main thing is that we maintain our friendship."

Destiny's Child ended on good terms. Each of the three girls wanted to go solo. They each felt like it was the right time to break up. After the last tour ended, they sang together one last time. They sang the national anthem in Houston. One last song in the town where it all started.

Family

It helps to have a great family. Beyoncé's mom is one of her heroes. Beyoncé told BeatBoxBetty.com, "Whatever I want, my mom is there for me." Beyoncé admires how everyone loves her mom. She hopes to be like her one day.

Beyoncé's dad is just as important to her. He makes her laugh and is very kind. She admits that these are two things she looks for in a man. She even wrote a song for him called "Daddy." In 2011, Beyoncé decided to start managing her own career. Even though her dad isn't her manager, Beyoncé still loves her father very much.

Beyoncé's sister, Solange, is one of her best friends. Solange has danced with Beyoncé at Destiny's Child concerts. She proved she has talent too when she made an album of her own music. Solange is also a mother. She gave her sister a great gift—a little nephew! His name is Daniel Julez J. Smith.

Beyoncé says she's always happy to see her family. They remind her what's important in life. They let her know when she does something good. They also let her know when she's being a little crazy. They keep her balanced.

Love for the World

Beyoncé worked very hard to get where she is today. But she's also had a lot of help along the way. She saw her dream come true, and so did her family. It makes sense that she'd want to give back to the world. After all, the world has given her a lot.

She sang a song with the rock star Bono to raise money for kids in Africa. She gives lots of her time and money to other charities too.

In 2005, she got help from Destiny's Child to do a special song called "Stand Up for Love." The song raised money for sick kids around the world.

Beyoncé performs at charity events all over the world. In 2003, she joined U2's Bono for a duet at the 46664 concert in South Africa. Organized by former South African president Nelson Mandela, the concert raised awareness of the devastation of AIDS in Africa.

In 2005, Beyoncé did a fashion show to help people hurt by Hurricane Katrina. The show had lots of famous people in it.

Beyoncé's family also started a charity in Houston. They worked with Kelly Rowland and called it the Knowles-Rowland Center for Youth. At first it was just a safe place for kids in Houston. But after Hurricane Katrina, it became more. The Survivor Foundation worked with them to give houses to people who lost their homes in the hurricane.

In 2005, Beyoncé continued her acting career as Xania in the film *Pink Panther*, starring Frech actor Jean Reno and American funnyman Steve Martin. Her fans eagerly anticipated her performance in *Dreamgirls*, the long-awaited film version of the Broadway smash hit.

Making Movies

Beyoncé enjoys making movies. She's good at it, too. A lot of people admire her acting career. In 2006, she got a **starring role** in the *Pink Panther.*

She also acted in a popular movie called *Dreamgirls. Dreamgirls* is a movie about three girls who dream about becoming singers. The three girls form a group called The Dreams. The story is a lot like Destiny's Child's story. Even better, the movie had singing and dancing in it. It was a perfect role for Beyoncé!

Facing the Future

For someone so young, Beyoncé sometimes feels old. She's been through a lot. But she doesn't feel like she's changed much. She doesn't think of herself as a star. She sees herself as a normal person. She can still laugh at herself. She talked to someone at *Film Monthly*, saying, "I like when people are silly because then I can be silly too."

In the end, Beyoncé wouldn't change her life. "I love what I do," she said, "I love to perform."

As a little girl, Beyoncé followed her dreams. Her creativity led her all the way to the top. Now her dream is a reality. She has a great career in music and now she is starting a family with husband Jay-Z. Beyoncé seems to have it all!

There are a lot of things Beyoncé didn't expect. Being a superstar isn't easy. But she would never give it up. It was worth it!

1981	Beyoncé Giselle Knowles is born in Houston, Texas, on September 4.
1992	Appears on *Star Search* as part of the group Girls Tyme.
1995	Destiny's Child signs its first record contract.
1997	Destiny's Child signs with Columbia Records.
1998	Destiny's Child releases its first album, *Destiny's Child*.
	Destiny's Child wins three awards at Soul Train Lady of Soul Awards.
1999	The album *The Writing's on the Wall* is released.
2000	LaTavia Roberson and LeToya Luckett leave Destiny's Child and are replaced by Michelle Williams and Farrah Franklin; Franklin quits five months later.
2001	The album *Survivor* is released and debuts at number one.
	Beyoncé wins Songwriter of the Year Award at the ASCAP Pop Music Awards.
	Destiny's Child wins two Grammy Awards.
	Destiny's Child wins five *Billboard* awards.
2002	Beyoncé appears as Foxxy Cleopatra in Austin Power in *Goldmember*.
	Destiny's Child wins one Grammy Award.
2003	Beyoncé becomes the first artist to have the number-one single and album on the pop charts in both the United States and the United Kingdom.

Beyoncé begins dating Jay-Z.

Entertainment Weekly names Beyoncé one of its top-ten entertainers of the year.

Beyoncé stars in *The Fighting Temptations*.

Destiny's Child receives four *Billboard* awards.

2004   Destiny's Child releases *Destiny Fulfilled*.

Beyoncé wins five Grammy Awards, tying the record for most Grammys won by a female artist, previously held by Alicia Keys, Norah Jones, and Lauryn Hill.

2005   Beyoncé and her mother begin a clothing line.

Destiny's Child announces they are breaking up.

Destiny's Child performs at Live 8 Benefit Concert.

2007   Beyoncé releases her second solo album, *B'Day*.

Beyoncé is nominated for a Grammy Award; Destiny's Child is nominated for two Grammy Awards.

Beyoncé stars in *The Pink Panther* and *Dreamgirls*.

2008   Beyoncé releases her third solo album, *I Am . . . Sasha Fierce*.

Beyoncé and Jay-Z marry in New York City.

2009   Releases a live album called *I Am . . . Yours: An Intimate Performance at Wynn Las Vegas*.

2011   Beyonce releases her fourth album, *4*.

Beyonce announces she and Jay-Z are going to have a baby at the MTV Video Music Awards.

2012   Beyonce gives birth to Blue Ivy Carter in New York City.

Discography
Solo Albums

2003	Dangerously in Love
2004	Maximum Beyoncé
	Live at Wembley
2006	B'Day
2008	I Am . . . Sasha Fierce
2011	4

Number-One Singles

2003	"Baby Boy" (with Sean Paul)
	"Crazy in Love"
2006	"Check On It" (with Slim Thug)
	"Irreplaceable"
2008	"Single Ladies (Put a Ring on It)"

In Books

Arenofsky, Janice. *Beyoncé Knowles: A Biography*. Westport, Conn.: Greenwood Press, 2009.

Bednar, Chuck. *Beyoncé: Singer-Songwriter, Actress, and Record Producer*. Broomall, Penn.: Mason Crest, 2010.

Gagne, Tammy. *Beyoncé*. Hockessin, Del.: Mitchell Lane, 2010.

Kenyatta, Kelly. *Destiny's Child*. Hollywood, Calif.: Busta Books, 2001.

Knowles, Beyoncé, Kelly Rowland, and Michelle Williams. *Soul Survivors: The Official Biography of Destiny's Child*. New York: Regan Books, 2002.

Knowles, Tina. *Destiny's Style*. New York: Regan Books, 2002.

Tracy, Kathleen. *Beyoncé*. Hockessin, Del.: Mitchell Lane, 2005.

Websites

Beyoncé Knowles
www.beyonce-knowles.com

Beyoncé World
www.beyonceworld.net

The Official Beyoncé Site
www.beyonceonline.com

Index

About the Author

Z.B. Hill is a an author and publicist living in Binghamton, New York. He has a special interest in adolescent education and how music can be used in the classroom.

Picture Credits

1: Dreamstime.com, Carrienelson1
6: Zuma Press/Rena Durham
8: WENN
11: KRT/ABACA Press
12: Zuma Press/Robert Hughes
14: Zuma Press/Ronnie Wright
17: PRNewsFoto/NMI
18: KRT/Adrienne Helitzer
20: PRNewsFoto/NMI
22: KRT/Nicholas Khayat
24: Zuma Press/Rahav Segev
26: KRT/NMI
28: UPI Photo/Terry Schmitt
31: KRT/Lionel Hahn
34: KRT/NMI
37: FPS/NMI
39: AFP/Anna Zieminski
40: Zuma Press/MGM Pictures

To the best knowledge of the publisher, all other images are in the public domain. If any image has been inadvertently uncredited, please notify Harding House Publishing Services, Vestal, New York 13850, so that rectification can be made for future printings.